World Issues

POVERTY

Kaye Stearman

Thameside Press

WORLD ISSUES

DRUGS
EQUAL **O**PPORTUNITIES
GENETIC **E**NGINEERING
POVERTY
REFUGEES

Produced by Roger Coote Publishing
Gissing's Farm, Fressingfield, Suffolk IP21 5SH, UK

Distributed in the United States by
Smart Apple Media
1980 Lookout Drive
North Mankato, MN 56003

Commissioning Editor: Jason Hook
Designer: Sarah Crouch
Consultant: Jim Mulligan, CSV
Picture Researcher: Lynda Lines

ISBN: 1-931983-26-7
Library of Congress Control Number: 2002 141372

Printed in Hong Kong/China
10 9 8 7 6 5 4 3 2 1

Picture Acknowledgements
We wish to thank the following individuals and organizations for their help and assistance, and for
supplying material in their collections: Care International UK 5 middle (Zak Waters), 5 bottom
(Jenny Matthews), 11 (Jenny Matthews), 15 (Dan White), 21 (Zak Waters), 24 (Georgina Cranston),
25 (Georgina Cranston), 28 (Dan White), 30 (Clive Shirley), 36 (Jenny Matthews), 37 (Jenny
Matthews), 42 (Zak Waters); Digital Vision front cover; Hutchison Library 8 (Nancy Durrell
McKenna), 35 (Billie Rafaeli); ICRC 3 (Michael Keating), 20 (Till Mayer), 22 top (Michael Keating);
Panos Pictures front cover main image (Clive Shirley), 9 (Neil Cooper), 12 (Clive Shirley), 17 (Peter
Barker), 18 (Bruce Paton), 26 (David Reed), 29 (Neil Cooper), 32 (Jon Spaull), 45 (Sean Sprague); Rex
Features 1 (Peter Brooker), 14, 34 (Peter Brooker), 46 (Ray Tang); Still Pictures 4 (Mark Edwards),
6 (Richard Choy), 7 (Gilles Saussier), 10 (Ron Giling), 16 (Mark Edwards), 19 (Franklin Hollander),
22 bottom (Hartmut Schwarzbach), 27 (John Isaac), 31 (Mike Jackson), 33 (Jorgen Schytte), 38 (John
Maier), 39 (Hartmut Schwarzbach), 40 (Mark Edwards), 41 (Mike Jackson), 43 (Shehzad Noorani),
47 (Mark Edwards); UNHCR 5 top (M Vanappelghem), 13 (M Kobayashi), 23 (B Press), 44 (R
Chalasani). Artwork by Michael Posen. The pictures used in this book do not show the actual
people named in the case studies in the text.

CONTENTS

Roxana's Story

Roxana lives with her family in south-central Los Angeles. In many ways, 15-year-old Roxana is lucky. She has a loving family and two parents living at home. She is one of the best students in her class and wants to go to college to study law. So, what's the problem?

THE PROBLEM IS that Roxana comes from a poor family in one of the most deprived areas in a rich city, and this will affect her opportunities in life.

Let us take school as an example. Roxana is an eager student, and her parents want her to do well. But the local schools are old and decaying. Roxana's high school was built for 1,000 students, but today it has three times that number. She says: "There are not enough books and computers, and classes are too crowded. It's impossible to talk to a teacher on your own, there are so many other students."

Who can study in such an environment? Not surprisingly, many students drop out – some join gangs or roam the streets. Some go to jail; some even get killed. Only about one-third actually stay in school to take their high school diploma. Yet, without this precious piece of paper, it is impossible to get a good job or go to college.

Even those who stay, like Roxana, have huge difficulties. To go to college, students must study chemistry. But while there are plenty of classes in subjects like cooking, floor-covering, and makeup, there are only a few classes for chemistry. It is difficult to get career advice and to prepare for exams. No wonder most students drop out.

Meanwhile, in wealthy West L A, students attend schools with small classes, good equipment, and interesting subjects. Nearly every student will go on to college, which their parents will pay for, and later they will get good jobs. Even if Roxana does get to college, she will have to work to pay her tuition and living expenses.

Roxana knows that her parents want her to have the opportunities they never had. She says: "My father grew up in a village in Guatemala where no children went to school, and many people never learned to read and write. Twenty years ago, he made a long, dangerous journey north. It took three attempts before he could cross the border into the U.S., and years of casual work before he found his job as a janitor. It doesn't pay much and the hours are long, but at least he has some security."

Although life in South Central is tough, Roxana's parents know that it is much harder in Guatemala. In their village, there had been no running water, no electricity, and no clinics.

About 60 percent of the people who live in South Central are Latinos – Spanish-speakers from Mexico and Central America. Many others are African-Americans, or from other ethnic minorities. They all face discrimination in education and employment. Even though they live in one of the world's richest cities, poverty affects their lives.

Poverty in three countries

Poverty is a major problem in many parts of the world, especially in less-developed countries like those below.

GUATEMALA
Guatemala is a beautiful country, but very poor. Many farms are so tiny that each year farmers have to travel to the coffee plantations to work. They are paid low wages and work in terrible conditions.

BANGLADESH
Most land in Bangladesh is very fertile. But there are many people, and there is not enough land to support everyone. So, each year people migrate to the cities where they can find work in clothing factories.

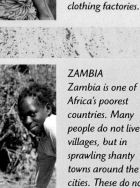

ZAMBIA
Zambia is one of Africa's poorest countries. Many people do not live in villages, but in sprawling shanty towns around the big cities. These do not have basic services like running water or garbage collection.

What Is Poverty?

We all think we know the meaning of the words "rich" and "poor." "Rich" means that you have plenty of good things – perhaps even more than you need – and 'poor' means you do not have enough, or perhaps any, of the same things. But how do we decide whether someone is rich or poor?

LOOK AT THE lists here. Starting with the first list, Your Things, decide what things are necessary for you to live a good life, what things would make you feel "rich" and what things would make you feel "poor". Are there other things you would add to the list of what things are necessary, and why would you include them?

Now do the same exercise, using the lists for Your Family and Your Community. How do the three lists compare with each other? Do you think that there are some things that every single person should have, regardless of who they are or whether they are rich or poor? Now, make your own list of the things you think are necessary, starting with the most important and ending with the least important.

Your Things

- A computer
- Books, pens and pencils
- A cellphone
- An ordinary phone
- A pair of trainers
- A pair of sandals
- New clothes every month
- New clothes every year
- Your own bed
- Your own bedroom
- An allowance for doing work around the home
- An allowance without doing any work

Rainy season in the city – and no way to stay dry in this crowded slum in India.

Your Family

- A dishwasher
- A car
- Two cars
- A donkey and a cart
- A bank account
- One or more credit cards
- Three regular meals a day
- One regular meal a day
- A television set
- A television set in each room
- Vacations away from home every year
- Vacations staying at home every year

Summer in the city – but a dirty alleyway must serve as a playground for these New York children.

Your Community

- Running water in every home
- Running water from hydrants in the street
- Electric lighting in every home
- Electric lighting in every street
- Regular public transportation
- Old and unreliable public transportation
- Regular garbage collection
- Free health care for everyone
- Health care you pay for each time you go to the clinic
- A good school, free and open to everyone
- A good school, where everyone has to pay fees
- A not-so-good school, for people who cannot afford to pay

Studying in Australia. The children in a class may come from a wide range of backgrounds, and some will come from much poorer families than others.

Is poverty different in different countries?

Jack from Australia and Abu Hameed from Bangladesh, in Asia, are both 11 years old. What do you think their stories tell you about being rich and poor?

Jack feels different from the other children in his class. They have lots of nice things – clothes, games, computers. His mother buys his clothes from the "op shop" (thrift store), and he uses a computer at the local library. His mother says not to worry – he is bright and is doing well at school. Still, Jack never invites other children home, and he wishes he had a room of his own. He feels it would not be so bad if everyone was in the same situation.

Abu Hameed belongs to one of the richest families in his village. His father owns ten *bighas* of land, and has two cows and a plow. His family of six live in a three-room house, made of concrete with a tin roof. They have a radio and electric light, although the electricity supply often fails. His mother draws water from the tube-well, just like everyone else does. Abu Hameed attends primary school and may go on to secondary school.

Who is poorer?

Jack has more possessions than Abu Hameed, and his home has electricity and running water. He knows he will go to secondary school. One day he expects to have his own computer, and maybe a car as well. But compared to the other pupils, he looks and feels poor – and he is ashamed of his poverty.

Abu Hameed looks and feels confident. Although he does not have as much as Jack, and has never seen a computer, his family is well off and respected by other villagers. One day he will take over his father's role as head of the family.

The stories show how poverty and wealth can mean different things in different countries. Poverty is about much more than what you can afford to do or buy. It is also about whether you feel part of society, and whether you can join in with other people.

Country contrasts

Australia
Population: 19 million
Average annual income:
    US$20, 540
Children in primary school: 100%

Bangladesh
Population: 120 million
Average annual income: US$220
Children in primary school: 70%

Father and son plowing the fields in Bangladesh, where a family with cattle and good land might be considered rich.

How do we measure poverty?

As we have seen, poverty means different things in different countries. What is regarded as poverty in a wealthy country such as Australia is different from poverty in a poor country such as Bangladesh. This is called "relative poverty."

The United Nations (UN) tries to measure the numbers of people living in the worst poverty – what it calls "absolute poverty." In simple language, absolute poverty occurs when people lack the basic things needed to live. These include enough food, safe drinking water, sanitation, healthcare, shelter, education, and access to benefits. The UN estimates that of the world's 6 billion people, about 1.2 billion – one fifth – live in absolute poverty. In money terms, these people survive on less than US$1 a day. That amount has to cover everything – food and drink, housing, clothes, travel, medicine, repaying debts, and emergencies.

Who lives in absolute poverty?

Most of these 1.2 billion people live in Africa and Asia, especially India, Pakistan, and Bangladesh. Around 70 percent are women and girls. Many cannot read or write. Most do not have regular income or employment, and when they do, their earnings are tiny. Most own very little – usually just their clothes, some personal possessions and a few pots, pans, and tools. If they are ill or injured, they must rely on their family to help. Many are in debt.

Let us look at just one of these 1.2 billion people – nine-year-old Namwinga from Zambia, in Africa. She lives with her aunt and cousins in a tiny, one-room home in a neighborhood called Chipata on the outskirts of the capital Lusaka. Her mother died two years ago.

These makeshift shelters are home to the families of laborers who build luxury apartments (in the background) in Mumbai (Bombay) in India.

Zambia

Population: 10 million
Average annual income: US$330
Children in primary school: 75%

Selling onions by the roadside is one way to earn money in Chipata.

Now her aunt supports all the children by selling vegetables in the market. Her aunt treats Namwinga well, but there is never enough income or enough food. There is certainly not enough to pay school fees for all the children. So, each day Namwinga stays home, fetches water, and looks after the smaller children. She will need to find paid work when she is older, but without schooling she has no hope of getting a well-paid job.

Some families in Chipata are slightly better off, and manage to save, move to a bigger house, and buy furniture and a radio. Although these families are poor, they do not live in absolute poverty like Namwinga. But often the dividing line is very thin – all it takes is an illness or accident to plunge a whole family back into absolute poverty.

This chart shows where in the world people in absolute poverty live, as a percentage of the total number of people living in absolute poverty.

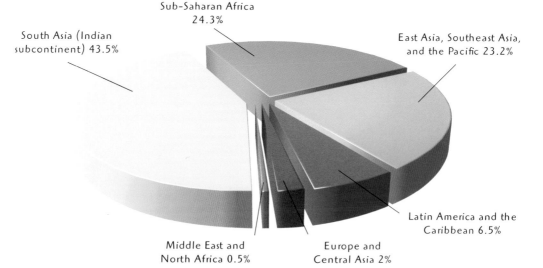

Sub-Saharan Africa 24.3%

South Asia (Indian subcontinent) 43.5%

East Asia, Southeast Asia, and the Pacific 23.2%

Latin America and the Caribbean 6.5%

Middle East and North Africa 0.5%

Europe and Central Asia 2%

Why Are People Poor?

Why are some people poorer than others? Is it because they are too lazy to work? Is it because they cannot earn enough? Maybe they have too many children or live in a bad area. Or is it just a matter of luck? What other explanations can you think of?

There are many reasons why some people, like this South African man, end up living in poverty and having to beg.

I N THE PREVIOUS chapter we saw that there are different ways of measuring poverty. Poverty in a rich country is clearly different from poverty in a poor country. But despite the differences, there are still things in common.

Almost everywhere, poor people come from families with a low or irregular income. In other words, if a child starts life in a poor family, he or she is more likely to grow up in poverty. Poor children eat less healthy food, live in crowded, low-quality housing, and are at greater risk from illness. Their families have little money for good food, nice clothes, furniture, books, toys, vacations and the other things that help children have a good childhood.

Poor families usually live in areas with fewer facilities for young people, such as parks, sports grounds, swimming pools, and clubs. There are fewer jobs and businesses, fewer stores and unreliable public transportation. People feel trapped and stressed. No wonder some people turn to crime, begging, and violence.

How are poverty and education linked?

A good education, leading to a well-paid job, is one way out of poverty. You might think that everyone has an equal chance at school. But a child from a poor family rarely has the same opportunities as a child from a better-off family. Even when schooling is free, parents have to buy clothes, books, sports equipment, and other extras.

In the poorest countries, many children do not attend school at all, or drop out early. In richer societies, all children attend primary and secondary school, and many go to college or university. But schools in poorer areas have bigger classes, less choice of subjects, and fewer books and computers. So learning becomes more difficult. And if children fall behind at school, there is much less chance that they will catch up later.

Of course, not everyone born into poverty stays poor. Many people strive to get a good education, new skills, a better job, or a move to another area. Many more benefit from changes in society – such as a booming economy creating more jobs, or government programs improving education. The world is full of people who were born into poverty, but have a better, more secure life than their parents.

Country contrasts

Ethiopia
Population: 63 million
Average annual income: US$100
Children in primary school: 32%

USA
Population: 283 million
Average annual income:
    US$28, 740
Children in primary school: 100%

A good education is an important step on the road out of poverty. These children are being taught in Sri Lanka, in Asia.

A "dole queue" in England, where unemployed people can line up to receive benefits from the government. In poorer countries, people who do not work do not receive this kind of support.

Are poor people lazy?

How often have you heard someone say: "Of course some people are poor. There are jobs around, but they don't want to work." How true is this?

Most countries have "safety nets" to protect people who cannot work. In richer countries, sick and unemployed people receive social security payments from the government, and retired people receive pensions.

But in many countries, poor people have to work for a living because they have no other way of surviving. They own little or nothing of value, they have no savings, and they get no benefits from the government. It is difficult to borrow money, because few people will lend it to them. If they do receive a loan, it comes with a high rate of interest, and

they must find a way of repaying it. The only safety net they have is support from family members or close friends, but usually they are just as badly off.

Are women poorer than men?

All over the world, the poorest women do the hardest work, for the longest hours and for the lowest wages. Often they do "double days" – working inside and outside the home. For example, let us look at Devi who lives in a village in India. Her day starts at 4 A.M., as she walks in darkness to the well to draw the water she needs for cooking and washing. Devi returns home carrying her heavy load, careful not to spill the precious water. Every day, Devi cuts the vegetables and grinds the spices for family meals. There is no gas or electricity, just a mud stove, so meals take hours to cook. She collects firewood, milks the cow, and sweeps the mud floors, all the time keeping an eye on the children.

Devi also works in the fields, planting, watering, and weeding the rice seedlings. At harvest time, she not only works long hours under the hot sun, but continues doing her "woman's work," carrying water and cooking. The women in the village rise earlier and go to sleep later than everyone else.

Devi works seven days a week. Her only holidays are when there is a saint's day or a traveling fair comes to the village. Devi is clearly not lazy, and yet the only things she owns are her clothes and jewelry. She does not even think of the future, or whether things will get better for her.

Half the world

"Women are half the world's population, yet they do two-thirds of the world's work, receive one-tenth of the world's income and own less than one-hundredth of the world's property."

Source: UN, 1985

No load too heavy – collecting and carrying water and food is considered women's work in a village in India.

Do poor people have too many children?

There are many reasons why people want children. Parents may simply enjoy family life, or they may want children to carry on the family name. It is natural to want children, but do poor people have too many? Is this the reason why they live in poverty?

In certain societies, parents hope to have many children. In rural areas, children add to the family income. They help out at home, work in the fields, herd animals, and look after younger siblings. But as people move toward towns and cities, families become smaller. City children are more likely to attend school, and school can be expensive for parents. Modern contraception means parents can have more control over family size, though this choice is affected by religion and custom. But city-dwellers, rich and poor, generally have fewer children than people in the countryside.

Not so long ago, many children died when they were babies or toddlers. They died of quite simple illnesses, from living in unhealthy conditions, or from hunger. Today we know how to deal with these things, through better hygiene, modern medicines, vaccination against diseases, and nutritious food. As more children survive, parents feel less need to have so many children.

Why do children die of poverty?

Today, fewer children die than in the past. However, there is still a big difference between children's health in rich and poor countries. In rich countries, almost all children can expect to have a healthy childhood and to reach adulthood. In the poorest countries, around one in four children die before they are five years old. Even when food and medicines are available, their parents cannot afford to buy them. These children die of poverty.

Many children means many helping hands, on the land and in the home, for this family in Cameroon, West Africa.

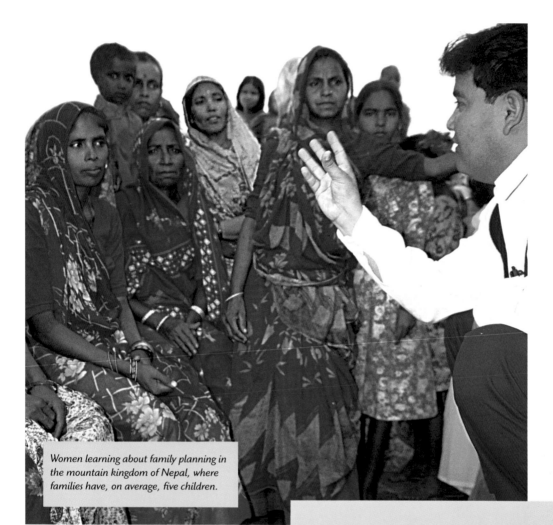

Women learning about family planning in the mountain kingdom of Nepal, where families have, on average, five children.

Birth rates are now falling as parents all over the world choose to have fewer children. This is true in rich and poor countries alike, although birth rates are still higher in poor countries, and poor people still have more children than richer ones.

However, having more children does not make people poor. They have more children because they are poor. If they become more prosperous, if fewer children die early, and if more children have the opportunity to stay in school for a longer time, then parents nearly always choose to have fewer, but healthier, children.

DEBATE - Should people be forced to have fewer children?

- Yes. Governments should stop people from having big families. More people means more poverty, and the world is already overpopulated.
- No. Governments should not interfere with families. If people want big families, that is their choice, even if they live in poverty.

Is Poverty A Worldwide Problem?

Organizations, including the UN, have studied whether the world is becoming richer or poorer. Although the answers are very complex, they can be summarized fairly simply.

THE WORLD IS getting both richer and poorer at the same time. More people than ever before have enough to eat and drink, live in adequate housing, get a good education, and live healthy lives. But there are also many more people than ever before without these things. While some countries have the means to provide every person with the good things of life, many other countries struggle to provide even basic needs such as food and clean water.

A large family in Ethiopia. Some of the world's poorest countries are in Africa, and the poorest people have the fewest resources.

A family in Germany. In the richest countries many children own computers and electronic games, and these countries use most of the world's resources.

Calculating the cost

In Ethiopia, in Africa, the average family has seven children. In the U.S.A., the average family has only two children. Does this mean that an Ethiopian family places a much greater burden on the Earth's precious resources? The answer is no. During his or her lifetime, a child in the U.S. consumes 50 times more resources (food, clothes, computers, furniture, fuel for transportation) than a child in Ethiopia. So, although an Ethiopian family is bigger, they use only a fraction of the resources of an American family. (See panel on page 13.)

As we saw earlier, around 1.2 billion of the world's 6 billion people live in absolute poverty. Most of these people live in Africa and Asia; some live in Latin America and Eastern Europe; and a few live in the richest countries.

Of the 189 countries who belong to the UN, the UN classifies 49 countries, about one-quarter, as "least developed." These are the poorest countries, who need special efforts to help them out of poverty. But, in fact, the gap between richest and poorest countries is so wide, it is hard to see how the poorest countries will ever catch up.

How is the world's wealth shared out?

The richest 20 percent of the world's people possess 80 percent of the wealth, measured in money and goods. This means that the other 80 percent of people must share the remaining 20 percent of the wealth. Even more shocking is the fact that the poorest 20 percent of the world's people own only 1 percent of the world's wealth.

There is another factor to consider. Many of the Earth's resources are being used so rapidly that there may be nothing left for future generations. Population growth and the rich world's demands for more and more goods take an increasing toll on forests, farmlands, seas, rivers, and oil, gas, and mineral deposits. And the worst shortages are in the poorest countries.

A family in the year 2000 faces the reality of starvation during severe drought in Ethiopia.

More than enough food

Today, the world produces enough food of all sorts to provide each person with 4 lbs. of food every day: $2^1/_2$ lbs. of grain, beans and nuts; 1 lb. of fruit and vegetables; $^3/_4$ lb. of meat, milk, and eggs.

Source: World Hunger, 12 Myths by Frances Moore Lappé, Joseph Collins, Peter Rosset (Earthscan, 1998)

What is hunger?

According to the UN, every day almost 800 million people – 1 in 7 of the world's population – go hungry. But what exactly do we mean by hunger?

Sometimes hunger is obvious, when rains stop, crops fail, and people begin to starve. We see television images of people with wasted, stunted bodies and large, staring eyes. This is the extreme face of hunger, but it is only part of the story.

The fact is that most of the 800 million people are not on our television screens. These people suffer from chronic malnutrition, a hidden hunger. They do not eat enough food, and the food that they do get is not nourishing. Without good food, children cannot survive and grow into healthy adults. Without enough food, adults cannot work and support their families. They do not starve, but they do not thrive either.

Is there enough food to feed everyone?

Worldwide, there is no shortage of food. In fact, there is more than enough to feed everyone. Whether we have food in our stomachs depends on how much food costs and how much we earn. All around the world, the poorest groups spend the highest percentage of their income on food, while the richest spend a much smaller proportion.

Over the last decade, the money paid to farmers for their products has fallen, yet the price of food in stores has risen. Often this situation is caused by governments, who pay lower prices to farmers to try to make them farm more efficiently. Farmers may become more efficient, but the more food they produce, the less money they receive for it. The poorest farmers have to sell their crops and animals simply to pay fees and taxes, and to repay loans.

Despite farmers receiving less money, prices in stores rise as governments cut subsidies on basic foods. Workers and small traders, whose wages have not risen, have to pay higher prices for foods such as rice, maize, and beans. Increasingly, the poorest people go hungry. The result is greater hunger and greater poverty.

In Bangladesh, hard-working farmers and fertile soil produce good crops, yet many people go hungry.

This boy in Rwanda not only tries to make a living by selling goods on the street, but has to look after his baby brother at the same time.

Does world trade cause poverty?

In the past most people were self-sufficient – growing and catching their own food, making their own clothes, and building their own homes. They did well in some years, and suffered in times of drought or flood. But today most people are linked to the wider world of buying, selling, and earning money, which is known as the market economy.

The market economy offers billions of people access to all sorts of different goods, many of which make their lives better. Even in the poorest communities, there are usually factory-made goods – such as clothes, batteries, and plastic buckets – some of which have been imported from countries on the other side of the world.

This mother and baby in Western Europe enjoy a world of wealth and choice. In contrast, many poor children in Africa face only poverty and deprivation.

Beautiful handmade clothing hides the reality of poverty for a young girl living in the mountains of Guatemala.

Seven-year-old Rosa lives with her family in a tiny mountain village. Every year, they migrate to the coastal plains to work on big coffee plantations. Wages are low and conditions are terrible, but it is the only way that the family can survive. Even Rosa must pick coffee beans.

Even when the world price of coffee is high, wages are low. But in the three years from 1998 to 2001, the world price fell by 60 percent. The growers now get less, and so do the coffee pickers. So, Rosa and her family face worse poverty. They will cut back on food; Rosa will not start school, and if someone is sick, there will be no medicine.

Surprisingly, the cost of coffee in the stores and cafés has not fallen. The growers only receive about 7 percent of the cost of coffee, while 93 percent goes to factories and retailers in rich countries. So, even while trade and profits boom, Rosa's family becomes poorer.

Most people earn money either by selling goods, or by working for themselves or others. But with many people all trying to do the same thing, competition is fierce. This forces prices and wages down, so people earn even less. Then some people cannot afford to buy goods, and this means that there is even more competition.

Is the market economy fair?

Often, worldwide competition is neither equal nor fair. The largest, richest countries have advantages – better technology, bigger markets, and lower transportation costs – which make it difficult for poor countries to compete. The most powerful countries also protect their own industries by supporting them with subsidies, and imposing tariffs to keep out goods from poorer countries.

Let us look at how world trade affects just one little girl in Guatemala.

The bitter taste of coffee

"Lower coffee prices are having devastating consequences for poor farmers in coffee-growing countries, while big multinational food companies, café and restaurant chains have gained enormously."

Source: Oxfam, 2001

Government spending in Uganda

1996

Debt Repayment:
    US$110 million

Primary Education:
    US$70 million

2001

Debt Repayment:
    US$56 million

Primary Education:
    US$140 million

Source: The Guardian, October 24, 2001

Is government debt a problem?

The poorest countries face other problems. Some are involved in wars that cost money and lives. Some have corrupt or undemocratic governments, whose rule benefits only a tiny minority. Even peaceful countries with democratic governments often lack the resources to make a difference to people's lives.

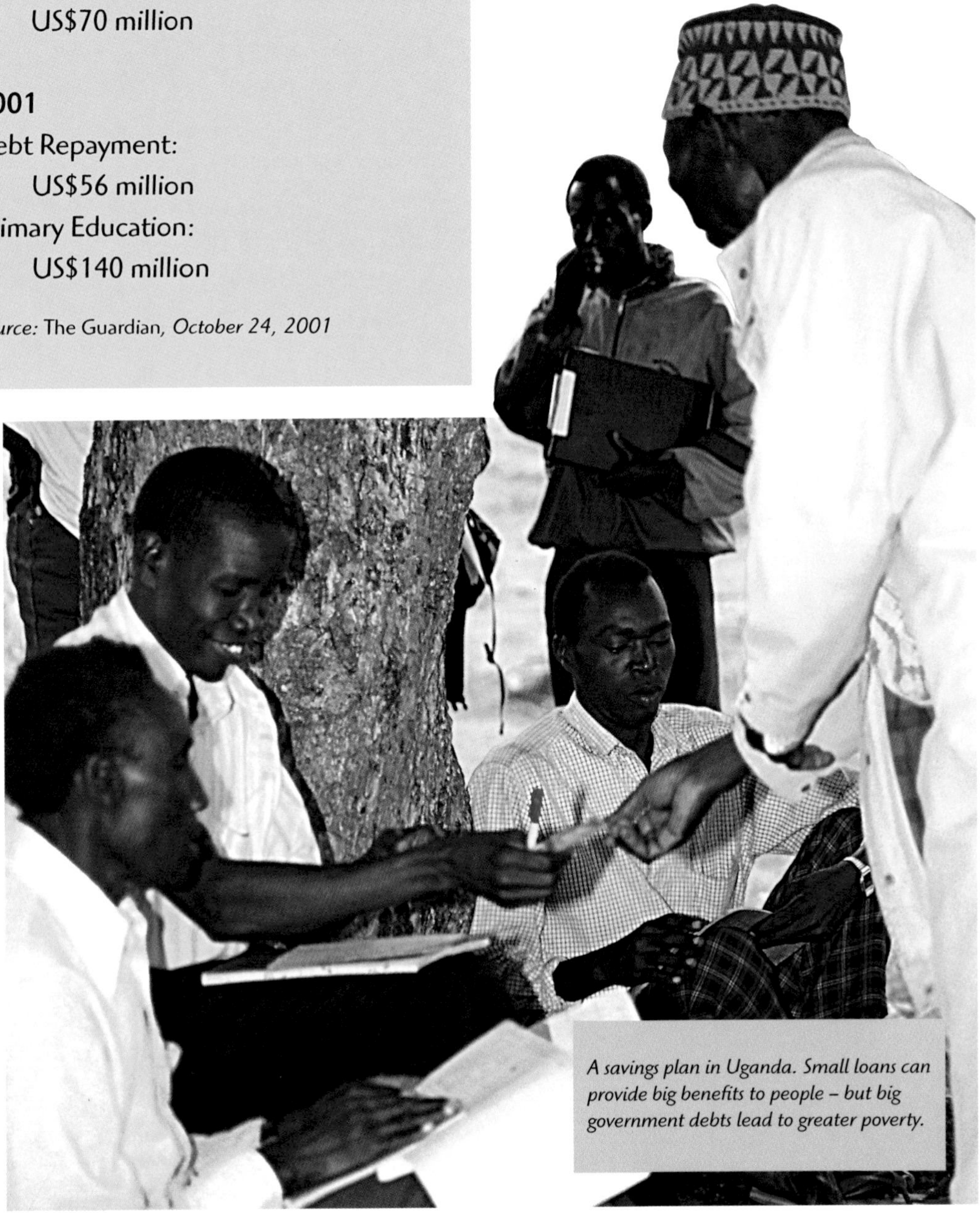

A savings plan in Uganda. Small loans can provide big benefits to people – but big government debts lead to greater poverty.

But one of the biggest problems for poor countries is debt – the money they owe to governments in the rich world. Many countries borrowed money 20 or 30 years ago, when interest rates were low. As interest rates rose, their repayments grew larger.

As governments try to repay their debts, they cut spending on areas such as health, education, and sanitation. This means that the poorest people miss out on the very things that could improve their lives.

How does government debt affect people?

One of the 49 "least developed" countries is Uganda, in eastern Africa. Uganda is a fertile land with hard-working people, but it suffered years of war and corruption. Then, slowly, things began to improve. Farmers grew coffee, and while coffee prices were high, the government was able to pay off some of the country's debts.

In 1997, the richest countries – known as the Group of Seven, or G7 – made an agreement with Uganda. G7 would cancel about 40 percent of Uganda's debts if the government would spend the savings on health and education. The government was delighted. It built 10, 000 new classrooms and abolished school fees so even the poorest children could attend. It seemed that Uganda was finally taking steps out of poverty.

But when the economies of the rich world became less successful, people started to buy less coffee. Coffee prices started to fall. Sixty percent of the country's earnings came from coffee, and it became hard once again for Uganda to repay its debt. All the work helping Uganda escape debt and build a good life for its people may now be wasted.

DEBATE – Should poor countries pay back debts to rich countries?

- Yes. If a country borrows money, it should pay it back, whatever the cost. If we cancel debts, governments will simply run up even greater debts.
- No. Poor countries can only repay debts by cutting services used by the poorest people. Canceling a country's debts gives it a chance for a new start.

A family enjoys the improved conditions in Uganda. The canceling of government debts allows the country to provide free primary education and better health care.

How Does Poverty Affect Daily Life?

Although poverty affects all age groups, babies and children are especially affected. Because they are small, they are more vulnerable to cold, heat, dirt, disease, hunger, and violence. And unlike adults, who can generally provide for themselves, young children are dependent for their survival on others.

POVERTY AFFECTS A person's health and welfare even before they are born. If a pregnant woman has enough food, a safe environment, and regular medical care, she has a good chance of having a healthy baby. However, if she lacks nourishing food, works long hours at heavy tasks, and has no medical care, she is likely to have a small, less healthy baby.

It is hard to stay healthy when you live in slum housing, like this family from Colombia, South America.

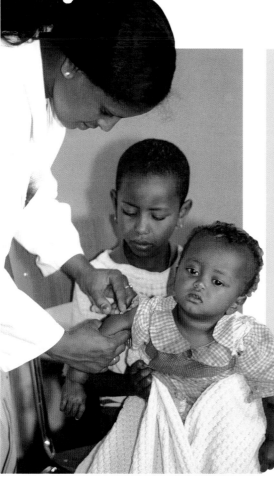

Losing lives

Over 12 million children under five years of age die each year, mainly from malnutrition and preventable diseases. Nine million of these children could be saved by using inexpensive solutions such as vaccination and antibiotics, which are in common use in other, richer countries.

Source: United Nation's Children's Fund (UNICEF), 2000

A baby girl is vaccinated by a nurse in Eritrea, in Africa. The vaccination will protect her against a range of diseases.

How does poverty affect children?

In poor countries, babies and toddlers die from common infections and illnesses, such as diarrhea, chest infections, measles, and mumps. In tropical countries, malaria is one of the biggest killers of young children. Sometimes there are simple, low-cost ways to deal with these illnesses, such as sugar and salt solutions for diarrhea, but medicines are often not available. The good news is that most children are now vaccinated against killer diseases.

Poor children are often malnourished. Not only do they not have enough food, they do not have the right sort of food with the vitamins and minerals needed for healthy growth. Poorly nourished children are small for their age and may have learning difficulties. Millions of children in Asia and Africa suffer from vitamin A deficiency, which leads to bad eyesight and blindness.

As poor children survive and grow, they face different dangers. Accidents are common, especially from hot cooking pots on open fires, and increasingly from heavy traffic. Children who drop out of school often take hard, dangerous jobs unsuitable for their growing bodies. Without education, young people have less opportunity to learn how to protect their health. This makes them more vulnerable to diseases and less aware of the potential dangers of "high-risk" behavior – be it taking drugs or exposing themselves to the risk of HIV/AIDS.

Work comes in many forms. This fisherman in India must spend long hours at sea in his small boat to make sure he gets a good catch.

How do people get enough to live on?

It is hard to be poor. As we have seen, poverty takes different forms, and it is often difficult to compare one country with another. But, wherever you live, poverty creates real practical problems in everyday life. The biggest single problem is always the same – being able to afford the basic things that your society considers essential for living. To do this, most people must work.

How do people make a living?

Most people look for a steady job with good, regular wages. But such jobs are not always available. They are especially hard to find for someone without a good education or special skills. Usually, there are many people all trying to get the same job, and competition is fierce. And even if someone secures a steady job, it does not necessarily mean they will be paid good wages.

Some people work with their families, farming, fishing, or herding animals. Others have to make do with what work they can find – odd jobs here and there. In cities, poor people work in factories, in shops, and on the street, selling everything from food and drink, to good luck charms and lottery tickets. Others offer services – looking after cars, carrying shopping, and entertaining crowds. Some people make a living by singing songs, playing music, or performing tricks. Others beg for money.

Work often involves traveling, but many people have to stay at home. This is true of women looking after small children or elderly relatives. Some use their home as a workplace, and this sort of work – known as home-working or out-working

– is often the worst paid of all. People need to work for long hours just to make the minimum amount, and it can be very lonely.

In some countries, poor children work as servants in the households of better-off families and receive no wages at all – just food and a roof over their heads. Most work very long hours, and some are beaten and badly treated.

Sometimes people get payments from governments, such as social security benefits or pensions, especially in richer countries. These can be vital in helping people to survive, but they are often quite small. In some countries, inflation has been so high that these payments are almost worthless.

Working together, like these women packing snacks in Bangladesh, can provide a better income than working as individuals.

How does poverty affect housing?

Poverty affects how and where people live, and their quality of life. Let us look at the stories of two girls – Luisa from Mozambique and Chloe from England. What do you think they have in common, and what are the differences?

Luisa is 10 years old and lives with her family in Polana Caniço A, a shanty town near Maputo, the capital city of Mozambique. The family shares a tiny, two-room home, very similar to the thousands of others crowded into this small area. Nevertheless, Luisa's family are very proud of their home because they found the land and built the house themselves.

Luisa was born in Maputo. Her parents had fled there from their village to escape war and hunger. When they arrived, Polana Caniço A was a small collection of makeshift huts. Now, thousands of people live there, and it has a school, health center, stores, bars, and churches. But most homes do not have running water or electric light.

In February 2000, fast-flowing floodwaters raged through Polana Caniço A, sweeping away buildings and gorging great gaps in the red earth. Luisa's family had to work desperately hard to save their home and possessions. Otherwise, they would have been left homeless.

Country contrasts

Mozambique
Population: 18 million
Average annual income:
 US$220
Children in primary school: 40%

United Kingdom
Population: 60 million
Average annual income:
 US$20, 710
Children in primary school: 100%

Raging floodwaters have gorged deep ravines in the poor neighborhoods around Maputo in Mozambique.

Growing up in Newcastle upon Tyne, Britain. Graffiti and trash are common sights in poor neighborhoods of big British cities.

Chloe lives in a public housing project in Newcastle upon Tyne, a big city in northern England. There is quite a lot of room for Chloe, her mom, and two brothers, and the school is near by. But look closer, and things do not seem so good. Inside, the house is quite bare, and there is not much furniture. Like almost everyone in the project, Chloe's mom rents the house from the municipal governments. The houses are modern, but they seem run down. Some are boarded up and empty, and a few have been burned out or damaged.

Most families in Chloe's project rely on government benefits. Many children grow up in jobless households and believe they will never have a job. Some turn to petty crime, vandalism, and drug-taking. That is one reason why Chloe's mom does not let her children stay outside after dark. The fact is that people do not take much pride in the area. When people do well, they move to better areas. Although the council is trying to improve life for the residents, most people just want to leave.

DEBATE - Should governments give more help to poor people?

- No. Governments help too much with homes and benefits. People do better if they are left to themselves.
- Yes. Governments should give poor people more help and greater benefits, to enable them to overcome poverty.

Does Poverty Affect Health?

What is the biggest single health problem in the world today? In 1995, the World Health Organization (WHO) tried to find the answer to this question. They came to a surprising conclusion. The world's biggest killer, and the greatest cause of bad health and suffering, was not cancer, heart problems, or HIV/AIDS. It was extreme poverty.

THE WORLD HEALTH Organization reported that the gap between rich and poor was growing, and so was the difference between rich and poor people's health. The poorest people lived shorter, less healthy lives. There was growing poverty in many richer countries. People living in the poorest areas often felt isolated and stressed, and were more likely to become ill. Although people had access to medicines and hospitals, they returned home to the same bad conditions.

The WHO reported that poverty had increased enormously in the former

A family at home in the former Soviet Union. Like millions of others, they have been plunged into poverty.

Learning about HIV/AIDS at school in Uganda, where the disease has already taken a terrible toll.

Soviet Union, where millions of people had lost their jobs as economies collapsed. In the past, people had depended on the government to provide cheap food and housing, and free medical care. Now, they had to pay high prices for the same services. No wonder so many people were becoming ill or dying at an earlier age.

How does poverty affect life expectancy?

The WHO found that the links between poverty and bad health were greatest in the developing world, especially in the poorest countries and those affected by wars and conflicts. Here, even having a baby is a big health risk. Each year, around half a million women die in pregnancy and childbirth. Nearly all of them come from the poorest countries.

Every year, 20 million people die from poverty-related diseases – tuberculosis (TB), which infects people's lungs; malaria, which affects people's bodies and brains; and HIV/AIDS, which by 2002 had infected around 40 million people worldwide.

Today, children in wealthy countries can expect to live to over 70 years of age. Contrast this with the poorest countries, affected by HIV/AIDS. Here, unless there are huge improvements, many people are likely to die before they are 40 years old.

This chart shows the difference in life expectancy between rich and poor countries.

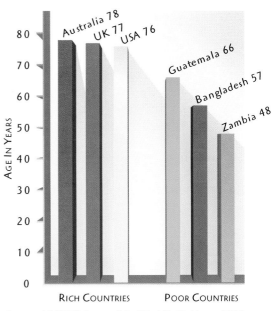

Source: UNICEF, State of the World's Children, 1997

On the streets. All the safety nets have collapsed for this homeless man living rough in the United States.

Does bad health cause poverty?

Poor people are more likely to suffer illness and injury than better-off people. But what about the other way around? Does bad health cause poverty?
The answer is complex. Not everyone with a health problem lives in poverty, especially where they have good safety nets such as a supportive family, a regular income, and low-cost, good-quality health care. But bad health can be a major factor in pushing people into poverty. This is especially true when society's safety nets are weak or do not exist at all.

Nick lives in the Midwest, one of the richest parts of the world. At the age of

56, he works as a security guard in a local shopping mall. It is not a great job, but it is a job and he is glad to have it. However, he is desperately worried about his deteriorating health.

When he was younger, Nick had a great life. He had a job, a home, family and friends. He earned good wages on the assembly line of a large automobile company. He married Tania, and they had two children. They were both working and could take two paid vacations each year.

Then Nick's company transferred production to another state, where wages were lower. He found a new job, but the wages and conditions were much worse.

One day he was badly injured. His past job had paid generous benefits to sick workers, but the new company gave minimum benefits. The family had to depend on Tania's much smaller wage. Before Nick could return to work, his company went bust, and he was laid off.

After becoming unemployed, Nick spent days in front of the television, eating junk food and smoking. He became overweight, and felt isolated and depressed. Then he had his first heart attack. The doctor said he should give up smoking, eat healthy foods, and lose weight. Nick tried, but he found it too hard to change his life style. Later he suffered a second heart attack.

Facing high medical bills on only one income, Tania also felt under stress and became ill. Nick wanted to work, but there were no jobs for older men with a health problem. Finally, he took the job at the mall, but he is very worried about his heart. He wants to be more healthy, but he knows that it is hard when money is so tight.

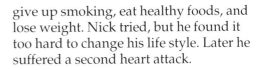

A widening gap

"In Scotland the death rate for unskilled men is three times higher than for professionals – a gap that has widened sharply in the last 20 years."

Source: Professor Richard Parry, Health Development Agency

Bad luck or bad health can force some Americans to exchange skilled jobs for unskilled labor, which pays much lower wages.

How can poor people stay healthy?

What does a community need to provide to help people stay healthy? You might suggest such things as doctors and nurses, hospitals and clinics, ambulances and medicines. Of course, these are important and necessary. However, it may surprise you to learn that the biggest single improvement in health comes from providing people with safe drinking water, good sanitation, and proper garbage collection.

Having clean water for drinking and washing protects people against germs and infections. Although this may seem obvious, scientists only realized the connection between hygiene and good health in the mid-nineteenth century. And even today, many people live without the conditions for proper hygiene. Why is this?

The simple reason is that poor people cannot afford to build or buy decent facilities themselves, and many governments and private companies cannot, or will not, do it for them. Hundreds of millions of people live in slums or shanty towns without running water, and use open drains for washing. They do not want to live like this – they simply have no choice. And if they get sick, they have to treat themselves or find money to pay for medicines.

Why is water so important?

Let us return to Namwinga, from Chipata in Zambia, whose story we looked at on *page 10*. For years, her family got their water from a local well. They had to line up for hours, and, what is more, they had to pay for each bucketful.

Clean, safe water in India – the greatest gift to support good health and a long life.

A safe water supply for Chipata, in Lusaka, has resulted in many fewer children falling ill from diseases caused by dirty water.

CHIPATA COMPOUND WATER SUPPLY SCHEME

Investing in the development of Chipata Compound

...ED AND MANAGED BY THE RESIDENTS OF CHIPATA COMPOUND WITH THE SUPPORT ...ARE INTERNATIONAL, LUSAKA CITY COUNCIL AND LUSAKA WATER AND SEWERAGE CO. ...JOIN THE SCHEME AT THE CHIPATA COMPOUND HOUSING OFFICE

ANNUAL MEMBERSHIP FEE – K 3,000 MONTHLY USER FEE-K 300 ...sed for operating and replacement costs, surplus for compound developments.

CARE DFID

They boiled water for drinking, but it remained dirty and could cause diarrhea and infection. In the rainy season, huge puddles attracted swarms of mosquitoes, which spread malaria.

Today, Chipata has clean water, pumped from deep underground and piped to 42 public hydrants. People still pay, but they make one monthly payment and get much more water. The water supply was planned by CARE International, an international aid agency, working with Lusaka City Council. Local people decided on the location of the hydrants and helped to lay the pipes. The water is cheap to buy and easy to collect. Best of all, it is clean and healthy.

DEBATE – Should people be given help to stay healthy?

- No. People should take care of their own health. They should save what money they have, and not expect others to pay for health care.
- Yes. Health is a public responsibility. Everyone should be prepared to pay something to help the poorest and sickest people.

Can People Escape Poverty?

Poverty has a devastating effect on the lives of individuals, families, and communities. Not only are people deprived of the basic things needed for a good life, they are unable to participate in many areas of society.

SO, IS POVERTY inevitable? Will some people always be poor, whatever the situation? We know that throughout history most people have been poor, and there has always been a gap between rich and poor. As we have seen, today's world has more poor people than ever before. However, there are big differences between our situation today and the situation in the past.

Poverty in the modern world – televisions in a shop window play on as homeless children sleep on the sidewalks of a Brazilian city.

Terrorist attacks kill children

One single event can have worldwide effects. On September 11, 2001, terrorist attacks destroyed the World Trade Center in New York, killing thousands and seriously damaging the American economy. Demand in the U.S. to buy goods from poor countries fell as a result. This lowered incomes and kept 10 million people in poverty. The World Bank says that, as a result, 40 000 children died from lack of food, clean water, and healthcare.

Attitudes to poverty – people rush for their trains, ignoring the homeless beggar.

Why should we be able to end poverty?

In the past, people lived more isolated, less connected lives. But today, we live in a world linked by fast transportation, and by electronic communication devices such as cellphones, satellites, email and the Internet. This means that a change in one part of the world economy can affect even the most remote communities on the other side of the globe, whether for good or bad. It also means that news – for example, of a famine – travels quickly around the world.

Today, we have the knowledge, science, and technology to overcome the worst aspects of poverty. As we have seen, the world already produces more than enough food to feed everybody. Even the poorest country has the potential to deliver basic necessities such as clean water, good sanitation, electric light, and primary education. Modern contraception means that no woman

needs to have unwanted children, and advances in public health and medicine mean that most babies should survive and grow into healthy adults. All these things suggest that we should be able to bring about an end to poverty, and yet poverty continues to affect the lives of millions of people around the world.

Why does poverty continue?

Although we have the means to make sure that everyone can have a good life, poverty is such a huge problem that there are no easy answers. It is not just a matter of giving money, but of changing how people live. Some experts say the problem should be tackled from the top, with more action by governments and the UN. Others think a solution has to begin at the bottom, with the actions of poor communities themselves.

The fact is that it takes action by everyone, including us, if we are to ever really make a difference to the problem of poverty.

Should governments do more?

We generally expect our governments to do something to help the poorest people. However, there is a lot of debate about exactly what role governments should play. One view is that governments should have only a small role, providing a framework to allow people to live in safety. The opposite view is that governments should provide a "cradle to grave" welfare service for everyone. Today, most governments have a role somewhere between the two, but it varies a lot between countries.

So, what should governments do for the poorest people? Should they help a lot or a little? Some people say that governments should focus on helping the groups who are unable to help themselves – children, the elderly, the sick, and the severely disabled. But what about other poor people, such as healthy adults? Do they deserve help as well? Some governments believe that such help creates dependency, rather than encouraging people to help themselves out of poverty. But it can be difficult for poor people to get started without some help.

How do governments help?

Let us look again at Chloe's family in Newcastle upon Tyne (*see page 31*). After Chloe's father left, her mother had to bring up three small children alone. Her mother would have liked to go out to work, but it was just not possible while the children were young. She had to rely instead on benefit payments from the government. When she did look for a job, the wages were so low that she was better off staying on benefits. But at least she had this safety net, and the security of such things as free health care.

American aid arrives in Cameroon. The U.S. government donates food to many poor countries – but does such help only encourage dependency?

To get a better job, Chloe's mother needs more qualifications. Ideally, she would like to be a teacher, but that would involve years of study. Instead, she has taken a job in a call center on the city outskirts. She has to travel some distance, but the work is flexible and the government still gives her part of her benefits.

Chloe's mom is eager and resourceful, like most poor people anywhere in the world. But she lives in a rich country that has a social security system and a strong economy. The poorest countries cannot afford to pay people benefits. Many depend on aid from foreign governments and international organizations just to fund their budgets.

Some rich countries give quite a lot of foreign aid, and others give much less. But not all the aid goes to the poorest countries. Also, when a foreign government gives aid, it often decides how it should be spent. The money might be spent on health and education. But sometimes it ends up being spent on luxury imports for the rich, and supporting multinational companies.

Growing up healthy in rural Bangladesh, with a good and varied diet.

DEBATE - Should rich countries help more?

• Yes. Rich countries should be more concerned about world poverty. They should give poor countries much more aid.
• No. Rich countries interfere too much in poor countries. Instead of giving aid, they should drop trade barriers and buy more goods from poor countries.

Should poor people help themselves?

If governments cannot solve poverty from the top down, how might poor communities tackle it from the bottom up? Organizations working with poor communities often start by asking people what the biggest problems are in their lives and how they think they can be solved. Sometimes, this has dramatic results and can help people to take huge steps forward.

But there are limits to the bottom-up approach. Poverty is such an enormous problem that it demands changes in the way the world is organized.

How do people fight poverty?

Let us return to Abu Hameed's village in Bangladesh (*see page 9*). While Abu Hameed comes from one of the richest families, nine-year-old Kamala comes from one of the poorest. Her family crowds into a tiny house that is at risk of being swept away in the annual floods.

They own just one *bigha* of land, and must work as paid laborers to survive.

Even so, Kamala's family is better off now than a few years ago. Although they work as laborers, they also have new sources of income. In the past they used their tiny plot of land to grow rice. Today, they also grow vegetables and herbs, and use fewer harmful and expensive pesticides. They also grow vegetables on the dikes – the narrow, earth pathways that crisscross the fields – and use the public ponds to breed tiny fish, which they sell to other farmers.

While Kamala's family has supplied the labor to help themselves, they have been helped by knowledge from outside their community. Special classes supported by CARE International teach poor farmers new methods of farming, and how to work together more effectively. One benefit is an improved diet – the fish and vegetables that Kamala now eats mean that she is no longer malnourished. Her family's higher income also means that Kamala can attend primary school.

Kamala's family now has a more secure life. But they are still very poor. Their livelihood is at risk every time the rivers flood. The very existence of Bangladesh is threatened because climate changes are causing sea levels to rise, which creates flooding. Some of this climate change is caused by pollution from richer countries. Kamala and her family will continue to be under threat unless we make big changes to our world.

Annual floods in Bangladesh submerge homes and fields. Climate change makes flooding more severe.

Can We End Poverty Worldwide?

Poverty affects the lives of billions of people worldwide. It involves complex issues such as employment, trade, aid, and debt. It requires big solutions, involving everyone from the UN and the world's governments, companies, banks, and charities, right down to communities and individuals.

WE HAVE ALREADY talked about the role of governments and some of the steps they can take to end poverty in their own countries. But responsibilities do not end there. Every government needs to look beyond their borders to the wider world.

Each year, millions of people immigrate to work in wealthy countries, often illegally and at great danger to themselves. Most send money to their families, and this is often a vital part of their country's economy. Millions more people would migrate if they were

On the move in Rwanda. Every year, millions of people leave their home country, forced out by conflict or desperate poverty.

Women in Morocco pay into a women-only savings scheme. Most will use the funds to start small businesses or pay for their children's education.

Loans for a better life

In 1976, the Grammeen (village) Bank of Bangladesh started to make small loans to poor rural women without land or property. The women used the loans to buy goats or chickens, or to set up as small traders. They used the income they made for food, health care, and their children's education. Interest rates were low, and loans were repaid on time. Today, the Grammeen Bank has thousands of branches, and similar schemes are run in 30 different countries.

allowed to. Helping poor countries to build more prosperous economies would not stop migration, but it would provide more opportunities for people to stay in their own countries.

How can banks help?

Private companies often regard poverty as being outside their responsibilities. But today the biggest multinational companies operate on a worldwide basis. They may have their headquarters in one country and their factories, offices, stores and customers in dozens of others. By shifting production from one city or one country to another, companies are responsible for creating or destroying thousands of jobs. Their decisions affect the lives of people too poor to buy their products.

Banks rarely develop services for poor communities. Billions of people go through life without accumulating savings or opening a bank account. It is poor people who find it hardest to borrow money and who must pay the highest rates of interest. Yet experience has shown that small loans at low interest rates have enabled some of the

poorest people to harness their own skills and enterprise, and use them to rise from poverty.

Often, new ideas to tackle poverty come from charities and organizations that work with poor communities. They learn from experience what works and what does not. The lesson for governments, banks, and companies is a simple one: listen to the people who really matter – the poor.

A demonstration in London, calling on the British government to cancel the debts of poor countries.

Can one person make a difference?

Is there anything that you, as one individual, can do about poverty? After all, poverty is such a big, complex problem it seems best just to leave it to others. One person, working alone, may not feel they can make much impact. But together there is a lot that ordinary people can accomplish.

The first step is to be aware of poverty, whether it is in our own community or overseas, and to make others aware of it. Democratic governments do respond to public opinion. If we express our thoughts and feelings loudly and strongly enough, for long enough, they do start taking action.

What is 'Drop the Debt'?

One example is the Drop the Debt campaign, a worldwide movement against the heavy debts paid by poor countries (*see page 24*). This movement started modestly, with just a few people writing, speaking, and campaigning about the issue. Later, as information increasingly showed the links between debt and poverty, more people became convinced of the need for change. They began calling on governments and financial institutions to postpone or cancel the debts.

Thousands, then millions of people, gave their support to the movement. Many wrote to, and met with, their political representatives. Some marched and demonstrated, and appeared in the press and on television. Eventually, governments began to act. A few countries canceled all or part of the debts they were owed, while others gave support to UN plans to reduce debt. There is still a long way to go, but today the issue is on the world agenda and will not go away.

How can I help?

There are many other things we can do as individuals. We can campaign for our governments to take action to enable people to escape poverty. We can call on them to offer the poorest people support in obtaining work, education, training, and a better, safer environment.

We can support charities that give practical help, and movements that campaign for changes in laws and attitudes. We can ask banks and businesses to include poor communities in their plans, rather than exclude them. We can buy goods, such as coffee, tea, and cocoa, where the labels tell us that the producers are paid a fair price. We can support enterprises run by poor communities, where workers are paid a living wage. We can raise funds in our schools and communities for good causes and campaigns against poverty.

There is a lot we can do to fight poverty, and there has never been a better time to start.

Women in India using a loan from the World Bank to build new housing. Taking their future into their own hands, they are also building a better life for themselves.

REFERENCE

IF THE WORLD WAS A VILLAGE

If the Earth's population was shrunk into a village of just 100 people – with everything kept in exact proportion – what would this tiny world look like? That is what an American doctor named Phillip M. Harter attempted to figure out. These are some of the things that he found.

GENDER
52 would be female:

👤👤👤👤👤👤👤👤👤👤👤👤👤👤👤👤👤👤
👤👤👤👤👤👤👤👤👤👤👤👤👤👤👤👤👤👤
👤👤👤👤👤👤👤👤👤👤👤👤👤👤👤👤👤
👤

48 would be male:

👤👤👤👤👤👤👤👤👤👤👤👤👤👤👤👤👤👤
👤👤👤👤👤👤👤👤👤👤👤👤👤👤👤👤👤👤
👤👤👤👤👤👤👤👤👤👤👤👤

AGE
11 would be under 5 years of age:

👤👤👤👤👤👤👤👤👤👤👤

26 would be 5 to 18 years of age:

👤👤👤👤👤👤👤👤👤👤👤👤👤👤👤👤👤
👤👤👤👤👤👤👤👤👤

63 would be adults:

👤👤👤👤👤👤👤👤👤👤👤👤👤👤👤👤👤👤
👤👤👤👤👤👤👤👤👤👤👤👤👤👤👤👤👤👤
👤👤👤👤👤👤👤👤👤👤👤👤👤👤👤👤👤👤
👤👤👤👤👤👤👤👤👤

COLOR
24 would be white:

👤👤👤👤👤👤👤👤👤👤👤👤👤👤👤👤
👤👤👤👤👤👤👤👤

76 would be non-white:

👤👤👤👤👤👤👤👤👤👤👤👤👤👤👤👤👤👤
👤👤👤👤👤👤👤👤👤👤👤👤👤👤👤👤👤👤
👤👤👤👤👤👤👤👤👤👤👤👤👤👤👤👤👤👤
👤👤👤👤👤👤👤👤👤👤👤👤👤👤👤👤👤👤
👤👤👤👤👤👤👤

REGION
58 would come from Asia and the Middle East (including 21 from China and 19 from India, Bangladesh, and Nepal):

👤👤👤👤👤👤👤👤👤👤👤👤👤👤👤👤👤👤
👤👤👤👤👤👤👤👤👤👤👤👤👤👤👤👤👤👤
👤👤👤👤👤👤👤👤👤👤👤👤👤👤👤👤👤👤
👤👤👤👤👤👤

15 would come from Europe (including just 1 from Britain):

👤👤👤👤👤👤👤👤👤👤👤👤👤👤👤

14 would come from North and South America (including 5 from the U.S.A. and Canada):

👤👤👤👤👤👤👤👤👤👤👤👤👤👤

13 would come from Africa:

👤👤👤👤👤👤👤👤👤👤👤👤👤

There would be no Australians or New Zealanders!

RELIGION

30 would say they were Christians (Catholic, Protestant, Orthodox, and others):

††††††††††††††††
††††††††††††††

70 would follow other religions or no religion (Hindu, Moslem, Buddhist, Sikh, Taoist, traditional religions, other religions, or no religion):

††††††††††††††††
††††††††††††††††
††††††††††††††††
††††††††††††††††
††

HOME

50 would live in the countryside around the village:

††††††††††††††††
††††††††††††††††
††††††††††††††††††

50 would live crowded in the village itself:

††††††††††††††††
††††††††††††††††
††††††††††††††††††

LIFE AND DEATH

1 person would be pregnant:

†

1 person would be near death:

†

POVERTY

20 would be extremely poor:

††††††††††††††††††
††

26 would just manage to get by, day to day:

††††††††††††††††††
††††††††

25 would live in bad housing:

††††††††††††††††††
†††††††

41 (including all the under-5s) would not be literate:

††††††††††††††††††
††††††††††††††††††
†††††

13 would be permanently hungry:

†††††††††††††

6 would own 59 percent of the wealth:

††††††

The 5 richest would all live in the U.S.A.:

†††††

Source: Dr. Phillip M. Harter of Stanford University School of Medicine. This is an adapted and modified version of his findings, including extra figures.

Think of it this way. If you have regular meals, nice clothes, a roof over your head, and a place to sleep, you are richer than 75 percent of the world's people. If you have money in the bank and in your wallet, you are richer than 92 percent of the world's people.

FOREIGN AID

In the 1970s, the richest countries decided that they should give 0.7% (7 cents for every $10) of their Gross National Product (GNP, the total income of the country) as aid to developing countries. In 2000, only four countries reached that target – Denmark, the Netherlands, Norway, and Sweden. Together, all rich countries averaged only 0.24% (2.4 cents for every $10).

FOREIGN AID, BY COUNTRY (2000–2001)

Country	Amount (millions) $US	% of GNP
Denmark	1692	1.06
Netherlands	3128	0.82
Sweden	1830	0.80
Norway	1286	0.79
France	4294	0.33
UK	4580	0.32
Ireland	243	0.30
Australia	1011	0.27
Germany	5120	0.27
Japan	13 289	0.27
New Zealand	119	0.26
Austria	470	0.25
Canada	1752	0.25
USA	9747	0.10

Source: Statistics on International Development 2000–2001, DFID, UK.

POVERTY IN A WORLD OF PLENTY

PEOPLE LIVING IN ABSOLUTE POVERTY (2000)

Total world population:	6 billion
Total living on less than US$1 a day:	1.2 billion
Proportion:	20%

PEOPLE LIVING IN POVERTY (2000)

Total world population:	6 billion
Total living on less than US$2 a day:	2.8 billion
Proportion:	46%

PEOPLE LIVING ON LESS THAN US$1 A DAY, BY REGION (2000)

South Asia (Indian subcontinent):	522 million
Sub-Saharan Africa:	291 million
East Asia, Southeast Asia, and the Pacific:	278 million
Latin America and the Caribbean:	78 million
Europe and Central Asia:	24 million
Middle East and North Africa:	6 million
Total:	1.2 billion

Increased Poverty in Eastern Europe and Central Asia

1987   1.25 million people in this region live on less than US$1 a day.

1998   The figure has risen to 25 million.

1987   16 million people in this region live on less than US$2 a day.

1998   The figure has risen to 98 million.

Average Annual Income per Person (1995)

Richest countries:
US$24, 400

Developing countries:
US$1,020

Least developed countries:
US$230

Increasing Income Gaps

1960   Average income for the 20 richest countries is 15 times the average income for the 20 poorest.

2000   Average income for the 20 richest countries is 30 times the average income for the 20 poorest.

In 40 years, the difference had doubled.

Education and Poverty (2000)

Adults in developing countries:
3.4 billion

Number of illiterate adults:
870 million

Proportion of men illiterate:
18%

Proportion of women illiterate:
33%

Poverty in Cities

1960   24% of the population of developing countries live in towns and cities.

1998   The figure has risen to 41%.

In 1995, at least 600 million city dwellers in Asia, Africa, and Latin America lived in "health and life threatening" homes and neighborhoods, without clean water, sanitation, drainage, or garbage collection. Over 90% of sewage in developing world cities is discharged into rivers, lakes, and coastal waterways without any treatment.

The Impact of HIV/AIDS

In 2002, 40 million people were estimated to be living with HIV/AIDS, with 95 percent living in developing countries. As a result, life expectancy had dropped dramatically in some countries. For example, in Botswana, in Africa, life expectancy in 1987 was 61 years. In 1999, it was only 39 years.

Poor Children and School (2000)

110 million children in developing countries have never attended school. Of these, 66 million, or 60%, are girls.

Sources: Figures from World Development Report 2000–2001; Attacking Poverty (*World Bank, 2000*); The State of the World's Children 1997 (*UNICEF 1997*); An Urbanizing World, Global Report on Human Settlements (*HABITAT, 1996*).

GLOSSARY

absolute poverty When people lack the basic things needed to survive.

average annual income The average amount earned by one person in one year, obtained by dividing a country's total income by its population.

benefits Government social security payments.

bigha A measure of land used in India and Bangladesh.

billion One thousand million.

charity A group or organization that aims to help people or provide a service without making a profit.

chronic Deep-rooted, persistent.

climate change Manmade changes in the Earth's atmosphere, resulting in rising sea levels and changing weather patterns.

community The town, village, suburb or neighborhood we live in, or a feeling of belonging.

contraception Methods used to prevent a woman from becoming pregnant.

credit card A card used to make a type of payment through a company.

democratic Supported by the people, having a say in government.

depression A sad, negative state of mind.

developing world Poor countries that are developing their economies and conditions. Richer countries are sometimes called the "developed world."

discrimination Treating people differently and unfairly, because of their sex, color, ethnic group, or way of life.

facilities Resources, buildings, or equipment that bring services to people.

foreign aid Aid given by one country (usually rich) to other countries.

Group of Seven (G7) The seven biggest and richest countries (Canada, France, Germany, Italy, Japan, U.K., U.S.A.).

health care Medical care, including clinics and hospitals.

HIV/AIDS HIV (Human Immuno-deficiency Virus) infection leads to AIDS (Acquired Immune Deficiency Syndrome), an illness in which the body's protective systems break down.

inflation When money rapidly loses its value.

hydrants Water faucets in the street.

interest rates The extra amount you pay for a loan or debt.

learning difficulties When the brain works slowly or unevenly.

life expectancy How long a person can expect to stay alive.

malaria A tropical disease spread by mosquito bites.

malnutrition The lack of foods necessary for good health.

market economy The system of buying, selling and exchanging goods for money.

migration Leaving your home, village, or country to move elsewhere.

multinational A large company that operates in more than one country.

op shop Australian term for a thrift or secondhand store.

pension A payment to an ill or retired person.

pesticides Chemicals used to help crops grow bigger or quicker.

professionals Educated people working in a profession, such as doctors, lawyers, teachers, etc.

project An area where houses are owned by the local government, and rented to people who cannot afford to buy their own homes.

relative poverty When people lack the basic things needed to live a good life in their society.

safety nets Systems that support people and stop them from falling into poverty.

sanitation Hygienic ways of disposing of garbage and human waste.

shanty town A town of roughly built dwellings, lacking proper amenities and often built on the edge of a city.

slum A rundown, overcrowded building or neighborhood.

social security Payments by the government to people who are ill, disabled, unemployed or caring for family members.

subsidies Money paid by a government to keep the price of certain goods or products low.

tariffs Extra taxes or payments.

trade barriers Taxes that a country uses to make foreign goods more expensive, and prevent them being imported in place of its own goods.

tuberculosis An infectious disease affecting people's lungs.

tube-well A pump bringing water up from deep in the ground.

undemocratic Not based on the wishes or votes of the majority of the people in a country.

vaccination A treatment that prevents diseases such as measles, mumps, and chickenpox.

vitamin A deficiency A lack of vitamin A in a person's diet.

voluntary organization A group or company working to improve society, rather than to make a profit.

wage laborers People working for a wage, usually on a daily basis.

FURTHER INFORMATION

BOOKS and MAGAZINES

Bangladesh: The Hawlader Family
(ActionAid, 1997)

Begin Again (on the effect of debt on children's lives) (Christian Aid, 1998)

Children in our Midst: Voice of Farmworkers' Children (in Zimbabwe) (Save the Children, 2000)

Children Just Like Us: Growing up in the Gwembe Valley, Zambia (Harvest Help, 1997)

City by the Sea: Urban Development in Mombassa, Kenya (ActionAid, 1998)

Earthquake, Famine, Flood, War by Paul Bennett (Belitha Books, 2001)

Families Pack (Children from the U.K., Philippines, Bosnia, Burkina Faso) (Save the Children, 1999)

Ghana: The Mahama Family (ActionAid, 1996)

Peru: The Aguilar Family (ActionAid, 1997)

Poverty by Teresa Garlake (Hodder Wayland, 1999)

Poverty and Health: Reaping a Richer Harvest by Marie-Therese Feuerstein (Macmillan, 1997)

Sustainable Human Development (Peace Child International, 2002)

The State of the World's Children, Annual Report (UNICEF, country offices)

World Development Report, Annual Report (World Bank, Washington)

World Hunger, 12 Myths by Frances Moore Lappé (Joseph Collins and Peter Rosset, Earthscan, London, 1998)

ORGANIZATIONS

Most countries have government and non-government organizations which can supply information and resources. Here are some U.S. resources...

America's Second Harvest
35 E. Whacker Dr. # 2000
Chicago, Ill 60601
This is the nation's largest hunger relief organization, feeding about 26 million hungry Americans each year.

Bread for the World
50 F St. N.W., Suite 500
Washington DC 20001
email: bread@bread.org
Christian charity coordinating church aid to the world's poor.

CARE
151 Ellis St. N.E.
Atlanta, Georgia 30303-2440
www.careusa.org
email: info@care.org
Care international is one of the world's largest private humanitarian organizations, giving aid to the world's poor.

Catholic Relief Services
209 West Fayette St.
Baltimore MD 21201-3443
webmaster@catholicrelief.org
Catholic charity helping people in over 80 poorer countries.

Food for the Hungry
7729 East Greenaway Rd.
Scottsdale, AZ 85260
www.fh.org
Christian relief organization.

Food Research and Action Center
(FRAC)
1875 Connecticut Ave. N.W., Suite 540
Washington DC 200009
webmaster@frac.org
Leading organization on eradicating
hunger and malnutrition in the U.S.

**National Center for Children in
Poverty**
154 Haven Ave.
New York, NY 10032
Website:cpmcnet.columbia.edu/
  dept/nccp
Publishes factsheets on child poverty in
U.S. and promotes ways of improving
the lives of low-income families.

One World U.S.
Benton Foundation
950 18th St. N.W.
Washington DC 20006
us@oneworld.net
Part of 1000 organizations working for
social justice on global issues.

Oxfam America
26 West St.
Boston, MA 02111
www.oxfamamerica.org

UNICEF
333 East 38th St.
New York, NY 10016
www.unicefusa.org

WEBSITES
www.worldbank.org
A massive source of statistics and
information from the World Bank.

www.jubilee2000uk.org
This site is a good place to start if you
want to find out more about the Drop
the Debt campaign to cancel the debts of
the world's poorest countries.

www.hungerinamerica.org
Hunger in America 2001 is a nationwide
study which shows the extent of hunger
in the U.S.

INDEX